MW01166641

A DEVOTIONAL FOR

The Restless Mind

A JOURNEY THROUGH SCRIPTURE TO IMPROVE MENTAL AND SPIRITUAL HEALTH

Copyright © 2021 Makenna Evers
All rights reserved.

Cover Photo by Gahan N Rao on Unsplash

INTRODUCTION

This devotional was originally for just me. I was going through a season of severe anxiety and I needed an outlet to connect with God on a deeper level. I began writing about the scriptures God put on my heart. As God spoke to me, I was encouraged, challenged, and refined.

Somewhere along the way, I felt God urging me to share my journey. I began to think about all the people who may struggle with anxiety, stress, or depression like I do. As a graduate student in mental health counseling, I have learned a great deal about the psychological and physiological aspects of mental health. Stress, anxiety, grief, depression, worry, anger, fear, and trauma are all things that can impact us psychologically and spiritually. Many psychological concepts emphasize the importance of healthy patterns of thought, seeing things from a new perspective, and productive coping mechanisms. As I began to integrate psychological concepts with Scripture, I gained a better understanding of the impact of mental health on our lives and our walk with the Lord.

Psychology illustrates the reality of mental illness and the brokenness of mankind, which reveals our desperate need for a Savior. The gospel brings hope to us and gives us the opportunity to know Christ as a Friend and a Deliverer. My goal is to integrate research about mental health with Scripture so that healing and growth occurs on both levels.

At different times in our lives, we find ourselves in the valley. I realized we have two choices in this valley: to abandon faith and try to do things on our own, or to draw closer to the Lord. Sometimes it may feel as though you do not have the strength to hold on to God. Mental illness affects millions of people worldwide. We live in a broken world with so much pain and suffering, but there is hope in Jesus. He is not blind to our pain. He does not abandon us in our time of need. The Scriptures I have included in this devotional illustrate that God draws near to the brokenhearted.

I called this book a *Devotional for the Restless Mind* because things such as stress, anger, depression, unforgiveness, and anxiety can invade our minds and plague us with relentless, out of control thoughts and feelings. A mind that is restless is unable to be at peace. My prayer is that as you read this devotional, you will discover purpose and peace so your mind can rest.

I pray that this devotional will encourage and remind you that you are not alone in your struggles. I hope that you will be lifted up, challenged, convicted, and ultimately cultivate a deeper relationship with God, our Creator and loving Father. Take the time to examine your heart and address unhealthy habits or ways of thinking in your life. Be brave and be open to a process of refinement that will enable you to live a life full of freedom and the joy of the Lord.

STARTING THE CONVERSATION

Before we dig into the Word together, I want to start the conversation about mental health. It is time we address the stigma. Whatever your experience or struggle has been, whether it is anxiety, depression, bipolar disorder, stress, guilt, anger, abuse, mood swings, grief, addiction, fear, trauma, eating disorder, and so on, you need to know that you are not alone. Millions of people worldwide struggle with all types of mental illnesses or emotional problems. You need to know that this is not due to a lack of faith, or because you are not a "good enough" Christian. I know so many people, including myself, who love God with all their hearts and still experience hardships.

Mental illnesses are influenced by several factors. It helps to look at things from a holistic point of view. Consider how biological aspects, psychological functioning, your experiences, childhood, relationships, current living situation, job, coping strategies, relationship with God, and support system all interact for better or for worse. When all of these biological, social, psychological, and spiritual factors are mixed, we discover what makes us unique, but also what can contribute to our struggles. Remember that we live in a sinful, fallen world that is full of hurting people in need of a Savior. With Christ, we can find wholeness, but it is a process. On our journey towards mental wellness, we will inevitably face stumbling blocks, such as fear, anxiety, worry, depression, anger, and addiction. These obstacles can be caused by any of the factors previously mentioned, and we often can feel like we are stuck in a pit with no way out.

Everything I have said is not to make you think of yourself as a victim. In fact, despite the seemingly insurmountable obstacles you are facing, in Christ we are more than conquerors because He loves us (Romans 8:37). The love that God has for us is so powerful that it binds us to Him as His children; a bind that cannot be broken. God sent us Jesus Christ to pay the price of redemption so that we can come to God freely.

God gives us His Word as a light in the darkness when we feel stuck and hopeless. No matter how painful the circumstance, how deep the loss, or how debilitating the illness, God's love is greater. Our God is greater. He never forsakes us, never leaves us, and never will. He can take our pain and our struggles and make beauty from the ashes.

I hope to give you some perspective on mental health and your journey with God. They are not separate. God desires for you to find wholeness in Him. The circumstances in our lives and the burdens we carry have a way of giving us tunnel vision, and we forget who our God is and what He is capable of. In your suffering, instead of retreating away from God with anger or disappointment, draw *near* to Him. The journey to wholeness begins with a relationship with Him and a willingness to grow and learn. You have to be open to let God address the sins and shortcomings in your life (we all have them), and be inclined to learn how to change. If you have a negative perception of God, I hope that you will learn more about who He truly is and how deep His love is for you.

I have structured this devotional in a way that I hope helps you gain a deeper understanding of Scripture and then learn how to walk it out in your own life. *Read* God's Word, *reflect* on it with the Holy Spirit, and *apply* it in your life through *prayer* and *action*.

ADOPTION

Read

"For all who are led by the Spirit of God are children of God. So you have not received a spirit that makes you fearful slaves. Instead, you received God's Spirit when he adopted you as his own children. Now we call him, "Abba, Father." For his Spirit joins with our spirit to affirm that we are God's children. And since we are his children, we are his heirs. In fact, together with Christ we are heirs of God's glory. But if we are to share his glory, we must also share his suffering."

- Romans 8:14-17

Reflect

One of the most important aspects in my walk with God was learning and understanding that through a relationship with Jesus, God calls me His daughter and welcomes me into His own family. I do not think we will ever truly understand the depth of this concept. In spite of my mistakes, shortcomings, sinful nature, lack of faith, and my wandering heart, when I surrender my heart and my life to Christ, I become part of God's family. This changes my identity from a lost and confused orphan to a loved and protected child. The use of the phrase *Abba, Father* reflects the most intimate and loving name of God that we use because we have been adopted. Although some may struggle with the idea of God as our Father, it is important to note that earthly fathers will have shortcomings, but God is our perfect, heavenly Father who never abandons or forsakes His children. In fact, God demonstrated His unfailing love for us by sacrificing His only Son to bear our sins so that the veil would be torn between us and God. The reason this is so important is because understanding your identity in Christ will completely change your thoughts and behaviors. Consider the differences between orphans and children with loving parents. Orphans are fearful, insecure, unprotected, and alone. The behaviors of an orphan reflect these characteristics, as they are vulnerable and strive to take care of themselves. Conversely, children with loving parents are secure, without fear, confident, and supported. Their behaviors reflect a secure relationship because they are able to walk in faith knowing their parents are there for protection and support.

When I began to see myself as God's child, the burdens were lifted off of my shoulders. I see the world differently now. I know I can trust that my heavenly Father is in control. Believing that I was safe, protected, and provided for changed the course of my life. During my suffering, I understood that I was not alone. Verse 17 is very important. Because we are God's children, we are heirs, meaning we share His glory but also His suffering. Never again will I suffer in vain or on my own. We serve a God that suffers *with us*. What other God would suffer for His children?

Apply

How do you live your life? Do you live with fear, striving to control your circumstances but ultimately being controlled by your emotions? Do you operate out of insecurity because you feel unloved or abandoned? Do you struggle to trust others? Do you carry the burdens of your past? This is the way an orphan lives. This is not the life God wants for you. Instead, God made the ultimate sacrifice so you can live free of fear and uncertainty. Living as God's child begins with surrendering to Jesus as our Savior and seeking to have a relationship with God as the Father. Through this relationship, you can understand the depth of God's love for you and become more secure and trusting. Then, your behaviors will reflect the confidence you have in God being steadfast and unfailing. You can make decisions in faith, serve God with joy, and have healthy relationships because all your needs are met by God. Finally, when you are suffering pain, grief, or loss, you will have a deep assurance that you are not alone, and that our God suffers with us.

Pray

Lord, I thank you for sending your son Jesus so that I can know you. Help me to understand who you truly are and who I am as your child. Forgive me for being fearful instead of trusting you. Please heal any wounds I have that make me act out of insecurity. Teach me how to walk in faith knowing that you will never fail me. Thank you for adopting me and for being such a loving Father. Help me to live as your child instead of an orphan. Amen.

THE SECRET OF CONTENTMENT

Read

"Not that I was ever in need, for I have learned how to be content with whatever I have. I know how to live on almost nothing or with everything. I have learned the secret of living in every situation, whether it is with a full stomach or empty, with plenty or little."
- The Apostle Paul, Philippians 4:11-12

Reflect

Our human nature can cause us to continuously strive to gain more from this world. Our society promotes the chasing of pleasures at any cost. We spend many hours of the day scrolling through social media, comparing ourselves to others who are prettier, richer, with better jobs and houses. It leaves us feeling like our lives are inadequate and empty. Sometimes, we can become consumed with jealousy, covetousness, and greed; it can taint our view of life and cause us to constantly complain and be unsatisfied. Even when we receive blessings, it is not enough. We want more. More money, a bigger house, a nicer car, a better looking spouse, better behaving children, a more successful business. What we have is never enough.

Paul did not live this way. He learned the secret after experiencing both highs and lows, being empty and being full. Paul learned the hard way that the only constant variable enduring all circumstances was God. The word *content* used here is the Greek word *autarkes*. *Autarkes* literally means sufficient to self; to be independent of external circumstances and independent of all people. Paul used this word to illustrate an internal contentment, not from his own will but from the peace of God. Paul conditioned his mind and his heart to bow to the will of God in every situation, so that he could experience contentment in any circumstance.

8

Apply

How do we get to the same place that Paul was at? First, we must recognize our tendency to strive for more worldly possessions and material things. Understand that contentment in every circumstance does not come naturally to us. We have insatiable appetites and a desire to pursue what feels good. However, when you have tasted the goodness and faithfulness of God, your striving can finally cease. That is the second step- experiencing and understanding that God is the only One who will be able to satisfy your heart. Through His Word and His Spirit, we can find true fulfillment and peace. When we get distracted by the empty promises of this world, we have to teach ourselves to come back to the feet of Jesus and remember He is the One who can still our minds and give us the love we are searching for. Then, whatever circumstance we find ourselves in, we can have internal contentment knowing that we are God's children and that He is our provider. Our satisfaction is no longer dependent upon our circumstances or our worldly possessions, but comes solely from the Creator of our souls. Rest and know that all striving and yearning will cease in His presence.

Pray

Jesus, please forgive me for chasing after the things of this world. I know that my heart wanders and becomes overcome by desire, greed, and jealousy. Forgive me for overlooking the blessings you have provided me. I pray that you would help me see that You are the only One who can satisfy my heart. I want to know more about Your heart and who You are. Remind me that my happiness does not have to be dependent on my possessions or achievements. Lead me in Your perfect will that will truly satisfy my soul. Help me to live like Paul did, fully dependent on You for joy, peace, and contentment in any circumstance. Amen.

THRIVING, NOT JUST SURVIVING

Read

"The thief does not come except to steal, and to kill, and to destroy; I have come that they may have life, and that they may have it more abundantly."

-Jesus, John 10:10

Reflect

There have been many times in my life that I feel like I am struggling to keep my head above water. My main goal is to just get through the day. My purpose is just to survive; just show up where I need to and take care of the things on my list. It makes me feel like I am trapped in my circumstances, whether they are good or bad. I operate at 50% or less because I am quickly spending my physical and emotional energy and not receiving. During this season of merely surviving, I find myself frustrated, empty, and hard-hearted. I operate out of selfish motives because my own well-being is all I can think about.

This is not the way to live.

Jesus is clear when He states the enemy's purpose. The thief wants to steal our joy, kill our spirits and destroy our relationship with God. He wants to steal all the blessings that God has given us. When we are focusing on surviving by our own means, we are enabling the enemy to have his way in our lives. We miss out on so many blessings and divine appointments God has set out for us because we have our heads down. We are missing abundant life.

Apply

What is an abundant life? It is the opposite of just surviving our circumstances; it is thriving in God's will. An abundant life is not characterized by material possessions or social status. Life in abundance is the result of a deep, intimate relationship with Christ. And from that relationship springs out the fruits of the Spirit: love, joy, peace, patience, kindness, goodness, faith, gentleness, and self-control (Galatians 5:22). Living life to the fullest is not dependent on circumstances. We can have the joy, peace, and love that Christ came to bring whether we are in the valley or on the mountaintop. The problem is, we look for life in this world. We search for things to satisfy us and to make us feel alive. That's why it often feels like we are just surviving. We are chasing the artificial high that the things of this world give us. We look for satisfaction in other people, our jobs, or our accomplishments. The truth is, it will never be enough. It is when we finally come to the end of ourselves that we see Jesus, hanging on a cross, only to defeat death days later, and we can understand that true life comes through Him alone. A relationship with our Creator requires us to lay down our lives, only to find life abundantly through our Savior.

Today, draw from His well of living water to experience life to the full and to never be thirsty again.

Pray

Lord, forgive me for looking for satisfaction and fulfillment in other people or things. I pray that you would help me to seek you first so that I can thrive, being full of the fruits of the Spirit. Thank you for dying for me so that I can live a life full of love and light. I pray that you would help me to not let the enemy steal from me any longer. Amen.

THE BURDEN OF SIN

Read

"If we confess our sins, He is faithful and just to forgive us our sins and to cleanse us from all unrighteousness." -1 John 1:9

"When I kept silent, my bones wasted away through my groaning all day long. For day and night your hand was heavy on me; my strength was sapped as in the heat of the summer. Then I acknowledged my sin to you and did not cover up my iniquity. I said, 'I will confess my transgressions to the LORD.' And you forgave the guilt of my sin."
- David, Psalm 32:3-5

Reflect

The weight of sin is too heavy of a burden for us to carry. The effort it takes to conceal and hide our sins from other people and the Lord will drain us of strength. Research studies show that the amount of will and effort it takes to continuously carry the burden of guilt, shame, and our secrets can actually take a tremendous toll on our physical and mental health. The suppression of such powerful emotions can have a devastating impact on the life and the relationships of an individual.[1]

Confession is surrendering to the Lord. Sometimes, we need to confess the sins we have committed to others, such as lying, slander, or infidelity. Other times, we need to surrender personal things such as doubt, fear, shame, or guilt. We attempt to control our lives by holding on to our fears or secrets so that no one will see them. We make decisions based on the things we are hiding so that what people see on the outside is a "model Christian". However, inwardly we are burdened with the weight of carrying our shortcomings.

To be a Christian is to fall short. Our walk with the Lord should be full of the confession of our sins and our secrets so that He can continually cleanse our hearts. I believe that our faith is inhibited when we try to act like a perfect Christian who has it all together. If we think that we have it all together, then our relationship with Christ must be shallow. To know Him deeply is to realize His glory and purity and recognize our sinful hearts.

Apply

Here's the good news: it is never too late to begin confessing to the Lord. If you don't know how or where to start, find a godly friend you can confide in. It takes courage to recognize the ways we fall short. Thankfully, there is no condemnation for those who are in Christ (Romans 8:1). We may experience conviction, but God does not condemn you. The surrender of sin actually enables you to become closer to the Lord. Take some time to identify what you have been holding on to that drags you down. It may be blatant sin, but it could also be doubt, fear, anxiety, unforgiveness, bitterness, or anger. Instead of keeping these things from the Lord, surrender them to your loving Father so you can walk in His freedom.

Pray

Jesus, forgive me for holding on to my sin. I pray that you would point out anything in my life that I need to get rid of, and that you would give me the strength to release it to you. I know I cannot carry this burden alone. Thank you for your forgiveness and your love. Amen.

ALIGNING YOUR MIND WITH CHRIST

Read

"Those who are dominated by the sinful nature think about sinful things, but those who are controlled by the Holy Spirit think about things that please the Spirit. So letting your sinful nature control your mind leads to death. But letting the Spirit control your mind leads to life and peace."

- Romans 8:5-6

Reflect

The state of your thoughts and your mind will dictate the state of your life. When your mind is set on fleshly, sinful desires, it leads to death. Sin invades the mind and destroys the hope and peace that Christ offers. The world offers empty pleasures and leads to disappointment and pain. When you choose to let the Spirit fill your mind, it opens the door to life and peace. When your mind is no longer controlled and overwhelmed with sinful and worldly thoughts, you are free to experience the gift of God's peace.

The door to your mind is only controlled by you. The passage says "so letting your sinful nature" or "letting the Spirit". That means we have a conscious decision to either let sin dictate our minds or let the Spirit reign.

Apply

What is your choice? How do we open the door for the Spirit when we live in a world full of distractions and enticing invitations to choose sin? It starts with creating room and inviting the Spirit in. Invite the Spirit by listening to worship, reading God's Word, or seeking godly fellowship. Surrounding yourself with spiritual elements will create opportunities to fill your mind with life and peace. The Spirit is a gift, given to us by Jesus after He left this world. It is a gift that has to be accepted and received. Conversely, how do we shut the door of our mind to sinful nature? This requires constant effort and deliberate choices. We must sacrifice ourselves daily. We must lay down our pride, greed, and selfish ambitions and pick up our cross. Denying our sinful nature creates room for the Spirit to bring life and peace to our minds. It is a worthy pursuit that will change the state of your mind and your life. A key part of fighting our sinful nature is being aware of it. Every person has their own struggles. My sin may look different than yours, but it will undoubtedly trap us and steer us away from the Lord. Spend some time reflecting on what sins are the ones that ensnare you the most. None of us are without sin. Examine your heart and your behaviors and ask God to point out the thoughts, emotions, or actions that lead you into sin and away from Him.

Today, remember that the choice is yours. Will you choose to be controlled by your sinful nature which leads to death? Or will you choose to pursue God by purposefully creating room for His Spirit to bring life and peace to your heart and your mind?

Pray

Dear God, forgive me for letting my sinful nature control my thoughts and actions. Help me to submit to you and let the Spirit rule in my heart and mind. Give me the strength to be intentional about what I fill my mind with so that I can be filled with your peace. Amen.

DO NOT WORRY

Read

"That is why I tell you not to worry about everyday life-- whether you have enough food and drink, or enough clothes to wear. Isn't life more than food, and your body more than clothing? Look at the birds. They don't plant or harvest or store food in barns, for your heavenly Father feeds them. And aren't you far more valuable to him than they are? Can all your worries add a single moment to your life?"

- Jesus, Matthew 6:25-27

Reflect

This Scripture has been one that God continuously brings me back to. Worrying seems to be my first reaction to most situations or circumstances. I believe it is one of my biggest struggles. I worry about myself, my family, an my friends. Unfortunately, when I begin to worry about something, it takes me on a downward spiral quickly. I worry, causing me to feel anxious and out of control, then I strive to control things on my own, which results in me striving to control things on my own, leading to more stress. When things do not turn out the way I planned, I feel overwhelmed and helpless. Maybe you can relate to this crushing cycle of worry, anxiety, and stress. Jesus knows about our human weakness to worry when things are out of our control. He also knows the negative ways in which we are impacted by stress, which is why He addresses it so clearly. Research shows that stress is one of the most common contributors to emotional disturbances. High levels of constant stress actually impact the brain in devastating ways. When an individual experiences stress, the brain releases the stress hormone, cortisol, that prepares the body to deal with the challenge. However, when a person experiences elevated, consistent levels of stress, the brain becomes overwhelmed with cortisol and is impaired in its normal functioning. An individual can then experience physiological changes that interfere with life. Additionally, the brain's structure can be altered, making things such as decision making and emotional regulation difficult tasks. Finally, these impairments in the brain and the body can contribute to mental illnesses such as depression, anxiety disorders, mood disorders, and so on.[2]

Apply

Why is all this important? Well, to begin, Jesus was very intentional when He asked if worrying can add a single moment to your life. In fact, He knew that the opposite is true. Excessive worrying and stress actually impairs your functioning and can cause devastating impacts on your life. Understanding the effects of worry and stress helps us to realize why Jesus talked about it so directly. Fear is at the heart of worry. Fear of the unknown, fear of failing, fear of loss, fear of being out of control. Our natural instinct to fear is to respond with actions to gain some control. However, time and time again God reminds us that He is the One who is in control. Knowing God as your Provider can change the way you live your life. Instead of being in a constant state of stress that can cause your body to become overwhelmed, you can walk with faith knowing that God is in control.

But how do we let God take the wheel? It begins with little steps of letting go, and acknowledging when we are overcome with fear. Every time you find your mind filled with anxious thoughts about the future, your well-being, or the circumstances you are facing, bring yourself to God. Express your fears, and ask God to show you that He is in control. Take steps of faith by letting go of what you cannot control. Focus on what you can control: yourself. Engage in self-care to help yourself unravel when you become filled with worry and stress. Dive into Scripture and learn about all the ways God has provided for His children in the past. Surround yourself with others who listen and validate your fears, but do not allow you to stay stuck in them.

Your worry may not disappear overnight, but before you know it, you will realize that fear will has less and less control of you. Look at the birds- look at how He cares for them, and consider how much more you are worth to God. Rest and know God as Jehovah Jireh (The Lord Who Provides).

Pray

Lord, forgive me for being so quick to worry and stress over things I cannot control. Help me to see that you are a loving Father and you will provide my every need. I pray that you would set me free from fear and you would remind me that I can let go and trust you. Amen.

THE HOPE IN REMEMBERING

Read

"I cried out to God with my voice- To God with my voice; and He gave ear to me. In the day of my trouble, I sought the Lord; My hand was stretched out in the night without ceasing; My soul refused to be comforted. I remembered God and was troubled; I complained, and my spirit was overwhelmed.
And I said 'This is my anguish; But I will remember the years of the right hand of the Most High.' I will remember the works of the Lord; Surely I will remember your wonders of old. I will also meditate on all Your work, and talk of your deeds"
-Psalms 77:1-4, 10-12

Reflect

The psalmist was experiencing what felt like inconsolable anguish and difficulty. He cried out to God but was unable to receive comfort in his suffering. He had trouble sleeping and praying because of the heaviness that weighed on him.
There have been times in my own life when the pain of my circumstances consumed my heart and mind to the point where I could not find comfort even as I cried out to God. My mind was restless, full of anxious thoughts that kept me up at night. My soul was overwhelmed as I could think of nothing else but my own pain and the feeling that God had abandoned me. Times like these make us doubt God and feel as though we have been forsaken.
The psalmist expresses his uncertainty during his time of trouble until verse 10, where the tone of the psalm changes as the psalmist's perspective turns away from himself and turns towards God.
The pivotal point for the psalmist is in the midst of his troubles, he remembers the miracles performed and the promises fulfilled by

God in the past. This is what brings him such comfort that the tone of the psalm turns from despair to hope.

Apply

Hope is cultivated when we take our minds off our current circumstances and remember who our God is! He is faithful to deliver us as He has in the past. The psalmist not only remembered God's goodness in the past, he also declared it. He spoke of God's works in order to set his mind on the truth that God is the same yesterday, today, and forever.

You may be able to relate to the psalmist's anguish like I can. You may be in a time of such pain, confusion and grief that it is difficult to believe that God will deliver you. You may feel abandoned because you have been waiting for a response from God and have become weary.

I say this to you: Fight to take your mind out of your seemingly impossible situation and focus your thoughts on times past that God was faithful to deliver you and work your situation for the good. Read about the times that He has healed and delivered people in the Scriptures. Remembering His power and His loving-kindness will give you hope for the future and the ability to find rest and comfort in His secure arms. Having hope will enable you to endure your painful circumstances now because you believe that God is a loving Father and is in control.

Pray

Lord, there are times that my pain is so overwhelming that I struggle to see your goodness in it. I pray that you would help me to take my eyes off my struggle so that I can see you are working through it. Remind me of all the ways you have delivered me and blessed me in the past. Do not let me forget your goodness. Thank you for being so kind to me in every season, and for never forsaking me when I need you. Amen.

THE GOOD SHEPHERD

Read

"The Lord is my shepherd; I shall not want. He makes me lie down in green pastures; He leads me beside still waters. He restores my soul..."
- David, Psalm 23

Reflect

Sometimes I have nights where my body aches for sleep, but my mind refuses to cease. A few years ago, I began to recite Psalm 23 over myself repeatedly until I finally gave in to rest. I wasn't sure at the time why the psalm was so comforting to me, but it was. It was as though each time I spoke David's words about God to myself, my heart rate would slow and my thoughts would dwell on the image of resting in pastures and walking along still waters.

It was later on that I learned more about the significance of being compared to sheep. I learned that sheep are remarkably emotional, timid, and vulnerable creatures. For the sheep to lie down, the shepherd must make them feel completely secure and at peace. The sheep have total dependence on the shepherd and the shepherd's role is to do everything he can to ensure the well-being of his flock. David understood these characteristics of sheep and the role of a shepherd better than anyone. Jesus later calls Himself the Good Shepherd in John 10. He explains how sheep hear and recognize the voice of their shepherd. Jesus also explains that the shepherd lays down his life for the sheep, as He does for us.

Apply

I pray that the psalm's poetic imagery comforts you as it has comforted me. In the nights that my mind is restless to sleep, I remember the sheep who are just as timid. I envision green pastures and feel the Lord begin to still my heart so that I can lie down and rest. I hear the calm waters and feel the Lord guiding me beside them, refreshing my soul. In that moment, I feel such a sense of security from the Good Shepherd that I know I can let go.

The more we learn about God's character, the more we can see that He is our shelter when we are overwhelmed. If you have experienced trauma, grief, abuse, or find yourself in fearful circumstances, I pray that you would learn to know God as your fortress and safe place. Know that Jesus is your Shepherd and He can provide you with such peace and comfort that your anxiety has to cease and you can be refreshed by His Spirit and His love.

Pray

Lord, I am filled with anxiety, and I need your peace and assurance. Thank you for being such a good, caring shepherd. Help me to trust that you will care for me and never abandon me. I pray that your peace that surpasses all understanding would fill my heart and mind. Amen.

THE GARMENT OF PRAISE

Read

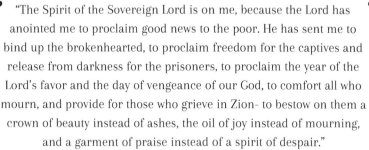

"The Spirit of the Sovereign Lord is on me, because the Lord has anointed me to proclaim good news to the poor. He has sent me to bind up the brokenhearted, to proclaim freedom for the captives and release from darkness for the prisoners, to proclaim the year of the Lord's favor and the day of vengeance of our God, to comfort all who mourn, and provide for those who grieve in Zion- to bestow on them a crown of beauty instead of ashes, the oil of joy instead of mourning, and a garment of praise instead of a spirit of despair."

- Isaiah 61-1-3

Reflect

When I read "a spirit of despair", I believe it is an accurate description of depression, grief, or emotional pain. There have been seasons in my life where I've felt heavy oppression like a thick cloak draped over me. When the spirit of despair is upon you, it strips you of all hope and joy. I remember being at one of the lowest points in my life and feeling like I did not have the strength to get out of bed because of the weight upon me. You may have experienced that too. What is so beautiful about these verses in Isaiah is that they describe what Jesus came to give us instead. What does Christ offer instead of the oppressive, lingering, heavy spirit of despair?

The garment of praise. Praise is an incredibly powerful weapon against depression. When we praise God, we lift our eyes off of our circumstances and express gratefulness to our Creator.

I tend to come to God full of requests and complaints. I have come to realize that I can become like a nagging child instead of a child full of faith and wonder. Instead of asking God for His gifts, uttering the smallest bit of thankfulness for just who God is can lift the heaviness off my heart.

Choosing to praise God for even the simplest blessings instead of dwelling on my feelings helps to lift the spirit of despair. Gratitude may not always come naturally. When we are in a deep, dark pit, it seems difficult to see anything other than our surroundings. However, this negative lens can be transformed by forcing your mind to cognitively acknowledge things you are thankful for. Even if your feelings do not line up, you can train your brain to create a habit of seeing things more positively if you make an intentional effort to focus on gratefulness.

Apply

Praise helps to calm our minds and still our spirits to find peace and rest in Jesus. I understand that there are times when you feel so weary that it is difficult to find your song of praise. Start small. Thank God for the breath in your lungs. There is so much to be grateful for, but we lose sight of those blessings when our eyes are fixed on the mountain before us. Let your praise drown out the feelings and anxious thoughts that try to overwhelm you. Creativity is a major outlet for your brain to experience stress relief. Create things with your hands, build, color, dance, decorate, take pictures, or collect things. These activities create space for your mind to take a deep breath and for your heart to praise God. Praise God with songs, praise Him with your words, and praise Him with your gifts by serving others. Let the garment of praise uplift your heavy, downcast soul as you fix your eyes on who God is.

Pray

Thank you, God, for all that you are! You are the Creator of the heavens and the earth, yet you care for me. You see me in my heaviness, and you offer a lighter yolk. I praise you for sending your Son Jesus to bear the burden I could not. I want to praise you in all that I do. Show me how to love and serve others in a way that glorifies you. Amen.

EL ROI: THE GOD WHO SEES

Read

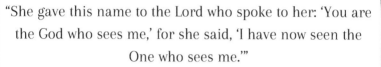

"She gave this name to the Lord who spoke to her: 'You are the God who sees me,' for she said, 'I have now seen the One who sees me.'"
- Genesis 16:13

Reflect

In our times of trouble, it is easy to become isolated and feel alone. When I am struggling, I sometimes think no one truly understands and I have to carry my burdens alone. In many circumstances, you may feel that you don't have anyone on your team; that you are facing the mountain in front of you with little or no support. When our circumstances are out of our control, we feel powerless and abandoned.

Hagar understood the feeling of pain and rejection due to circumstances that were out of her control. She was a slave, bound to do whatever her masters asked of her. Sarai forced Hagar to bear Abram's child as a way of trying to control God's promise to them. Hagar had to comply with her request and when she became pregnant, she struggled with feelings of pain and anger towards Sarai. When tensions rose between Sarai and Hagar, she ran away. Hagar was found by an Angel of the Lord, alone in the wilderness. The Angel acknowledged her situation and made her feel seen and understood. The Angel gave her instructions to return and promised that her situation was in the hands of the Lord. Hagar proclaimed that she met the God who sees her in all her pain and misery, alone in the wilderness, carrying a burden alone.

Apply

The God who saw Hagar in her pain so many years ago is the same God who sees you today. He sees you in the valley and He sees you on the mountain. He sees the pain you carry and offers a lighter yolk. He sees the hard work you feel goes unnoticed and reminds you it is not in vain. He sees you in your isolation and calls you home as a child of God. God draws near to the brokenhearted, the orphans, the widows, the outcast, the misunderstood, and the rejected.

No matter how you feel at the moment, El Roi, the God who sees, is there in the midst of your pain and trials. You are not alone, abandoned, or rejected. God is with you and He is for you. He hears your anxious thoughts and calls you to lift your eyes to see Him. Not only is Hagar seen by God, but she is able to see and experience Him as well. Hagar's experience with God and her new understanding of being seen and known by Him empowered her to return to her stressful situation with confidence. The veil has been torn; God is not hidden from us. Look upon El Roi, your Savior, your Friend, and know that He sees you and He is with you. Understanding that your life is held by God, the Creator of the heavens and the earth, can give you strength to face the mountain ahead of you because you know that you are not alone in your fight. If you have not encountered God in this way, He calls you to knock, and promises the door will be open to you.

Pray

Dear God, there are times that I feel so alone and overlooked. I often feel that no one notices the sacrifices I make or all the work that I do. But just like Hagar, I know you see me. I pray that you would help me to understand you are always with me, and that I am never truly alone. Thank you for never overlooking those who are rejected. You are a good Father. Amen.

JESUS & THE BLIND MAN

Read

"As Jesus was walking along, he saw a man who had been blind from birth. 'Rabbi,' his disciples asked him, 'why was this man born blind? Was it because of his own sins or his parents' sins?' 'It was not because of his sins or his parents' sins,' Jesus answered. 'This happened so the power of God could be seen in him.'"

- John 9:1-3

Reflect

Oftentimes, I come to God asking why I have to walk through trials and hardships. If I become caught up in questioning God, I become filled with anger, disappointment, and bitterness. It is hard to refrain from wondering at times why God doesn't automatically deliver us when we ask.

In Jesus' time, the Jews associated blindness (and other kinds of suffering) with sin and punishment. As Jesus and His disciples walked past a man who was blind since birth, the disciples asked who had sinned to cause the blindness. The first time I read this passage, I was struck by Jesus' answer. Jesus responded simply that no one's sin had caused the blindness, but the man's blindness served a bigger purpose. The purpose was so that the works and power of God could be displayed in him.

Jesus goes on to heal the man and the miracle stuns the people. The man now has a powerful testimony that proclaims the power of God. He spent his entire life blind, suffering and believing it was due to sin. When Jesus comes, it is as if all the pieces fall into place. The moment that Jesus healed the man, he became undeniable evidence of the power of God.

The same is true in our own lives. We live in a broken, sinful world. Jesus Himself told us that we will experience trouble. But your suffering and your pain can serve a greater purpose. God's faithfulness and His power is displayed in your life and in your hardships. Many people are hopeless in their suffering, and your testimony of having hope in Jesus despite your circumstances is powerful. Many people wonder what they have done to cause their suffering, but you can testify that God has a greater purpose and will work things for the good.

Apply

As you wait for God to deliver, heal, or work in your life, don't become bitter or impatient because He isn't working the way you want Him to. Take great joy in knowing that your hardships serve a greater purpose; even now you can be evidence of the power of God. When you catch yourself wondering "why?", have faith! God is always working, even if we don't see it. Your testimony is a powerful weapon, even when you are in the midst of struggles.

Some of the greatest blessings I have received is when I saw the purpose behind my pain. Although I have struggled so many years with depression and anxiety, it becomes worth it to me when I can offer hope to others who have a similar struggle with my testimony. There is a greater purpose. Your struggle is not in vain. The man lived his entire life blind, begging on the streets, and in a moment, God made him to be a living testimony of the power of Christ. Hold firmly to your faith today as you wait for God.

Pray

God, forgive me for not understanding that you are always working, even when I do not see it. I pray that you would soften my heart in my pain so that I can see there is a purpose, and you work all things for the good. Give me the strength to share my story with others and encourage them. Amen.

A TRANSFORMED MIND

Read

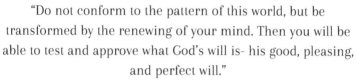

"Do not conform to the pattern of this world, but be transformed by the renewing of your mind. Then you will be able to test and approve what God's will is- his good, pleasing, and perfect will."
- Romans 12:2

Reflect

The condition of your mind has so much to do with the condition of your life and your relationships. This Scripture is a direct instruction to not be conformed to this world but to be transformed by renewing our minds. First, we must separate our minds and our hearts from the pattern of this world. The ways of this world are full of greed, lust, pride, adultery, deceit, and darkness. John says in 1 John 2:16 that the desires of the flesh, eyes, and pride in possessions do not come from the Father but from the world. While we cannot escape some of the ways of our culture, our heart does not have to belong to this world. Our minds do not have to be dictated by worldly desires and sinful thoughts.

The renewal of the mind is not just a biblical concept; it is a scientific idea as well. Recent research in neuroscience reveals how the mind can literally be rewired by creating new neural pathways and connections. This process is called neurogenesis.[3] What does this mean for us? It means that when we become new creations in Christ, we can truly transform our minds and change the way we think. Unhealthy neural pathways can be a result of several factors: trauma, harmful interactions or experiences, or constant negative feelings.

However, neurogenesis means that we can be set free from twisted thinking, harmful cognitive distortions, and other patterns of thoughts that can cause anxiety, depression, and other mental health problems. We can be delivered from a victim mentality and teach our brains to respond to situations and operate out of the mindset of a conqueror in Christ.

Apply

But how does this happen? Transformation is a process. You cannot rewire your brain in a day. The journey begins with conscious decisions to immerse your heart and your mind in the Word of God. Hebrews 4:12 states, "For the word of God is alive and active. Sharper than any double-edged sword, it penetrates even to the dividing soul and spirit, joints and marrow; it judges the thoughts and attitudes of the heart."

The Word of God is the ultimate authority in our lives. According to Hebrews, it cuts deep into our soul and it judges our thoughts and attitudes. Through study and application, the directions and encouragement we receive from the Bible will transform our ways of thinking and our behaviors. God's words speak directly into our lives and will give us a lens in which to see things from His perspective. The Scriptures teach us about the character of God and cultivates a relationship with Him. To rewire our brain, we have to break the unhealthy neural pathways and replace them with healthy connections resulting from an understanding of the Word and a connection with God.

A renewed mind leads to a life filled with the Spirit and overflowing with love, joy, and peace. The mind that is bound to the world experiences nothing but darkness. Strive to renew your mind with God's Word to walk in His perfect and pleasing will.

Pray

Lord, I pray for a newness in my mind and in my life. I thank you for sending Jesus to sacrifice for me so that I can become a new creation. Help me to read your Word and let it show me new ways of thinking and acting. Thank you for offering me freedom. Amen.

DAY THIRTEEN

JESUS & THE TEN LEPERS

Read

"As he [Jesus] entered a village there, ten men with leprosy stood at a
distance, crying out, 'Jesus, Master, have mercy on us!' He looked at
them and said, 'Go show yourselves to the priests.' And as they went
they were cleansed of their leprosy.
One of them, when he saw that he was healed, he came back to Jesus
shouting, 'Praise God!' He fell to the ground at Jesus' feet, thanking
him for what he had done. This man was a Samaritan. Jesus asked,
'Didn't I heal ten men? Where are the other nine? Has no one
returned to give glory to God except this foreigner?' And Jesus said to
the man, 'Stand up and go. Your faith has healed you.'"
- Luke 17:11-19

Reflect

There have been times in my life when I wanted so badly to be
healed, delivered, or rescued from my circumstances. Pain has a way
of demanding all our attention. Our thoughts and feelings revolve
around the pain, discomfort, and the need to be healed. I admit that I
have been impatient and discouraged during times that I have
waited on God. I have been so obsessed with needing healing in a
specific way that it governs my relationship with the Lord. When we
get in a place of only wanting the gifts of God without a relationship
with Him, we are robbed of all the blessings and freedom that comes
from knowing Him intimately.

As Jesus headed towards Jerusalem, He encountered ten men who
had been tormented by leprosy, an unforgiving and hopeless
condition. The men likely suffered on a daily basis, outcasted from
the village and left alone to waste away. Knowing the power that Jesus
possessed, they begged Him to cleanse them of their condition.

31

Jesus did, but astonishingly, only one returned to praise God and thank Jesus for what He had done. Can you imagine? These men suffered so greatly, and in a moment the Son of God came and healed them. They were free to return to their families and live a normal life. Jesus performed a great miracle in their lives, yet only one of the men returned. What Jesus said to the man who returned carries great significance. Because the man came back with thankfulness in his heart and praise for God, Jesus told him that his faith has made him well. We know that the man had already been healed of leprosy, but his response that was full of faith healed him spiritually.

Apply

When we are in times of great pain, physically or mentally, all we want is to be made well. We know God to be our Healer, and we know that He is able. You may have waited a long time to be healed. You may still be waiting. What we will miss if we focus on physical healing is what Christ also offers: spiritual wholeness. While physical healing is important and God is certainly capable, we cannot lose sight of the true treasure of being well spiritually. Accepting Christ into our hearts makes us spiritually whole and has an eternal impact. The man who returned to Jesus was full of faith and thanksgiving, a key to receiving true healing.

Decide whether you want to be the nine who received the blessing and left, or the one who returned with thankfulness and received an even greater gift. Faith and thankfulness can lead to physical or mental healing, but it also opens the door for a deep, true spiritual healing. Do not lose sight of your relationship with God as you wait for Him to deliver you from whatever your circumstance is. God is more than just the gifts He gives; He is a kind, loving, patient Father who desires for you to be set free through a relationship with Him.

Pray

Jesus, I thank you that you are our Healer! I thank you that you love us enough to work in amazing ways in our lives. Thank you for the incredible gift of eternal life. I pray for physical healing, but I pray that I would not let me dwell on what I want. I pray that you would help me to always be thankful, even when you don't answer me the way I want you to. Thank you for being such a good Father. Amen.

DAY FOURTEEN

FOCUSED ATTENTION

Read

"Fixing our eyes on Jesus, the pioneer and perfecter of faith. For the joy set before him he endured the cross, scorning its shame, and sat down at the right hand of the throne of God. Consider him who endured such opposition from sinners, so that you will not grow weary and lose heart."
- Hebrews 12:2-3

Reflect

There is power in what we focus on. I have found that in the seasons I struggle with depression, I have a hard time focusing on anything but my aches, pains, and downcast feelings. It's as if I am in a deep, dark valley and I can't see anything but the walls closing in on me. I feel too weary to continue on.

I have also found that the times when I feel the strongest is when I have my eyes fixed on Jesus. When I am focused on Jesus, my relationship with Him grows deeper and I feel as though I am on a rock that cannot be shaken. Everything else fades away, and I am encouraged and renewed by God's presence.

Why is there such a big difference in me depending on what I am focused on? Research on the brain reveals a possible answer. According to recent research, focused attention leads to the reshaping of the brain. The physical architecture of the brain actually changes according to where we are directing our attention and what we practice doing.[4]

Recall the story of Peter out on the lake on a boat. Jesus walks out onto the lake to meet them. The disciples were afraid, but Jesus called out to Peter and asked him to come walk out onto the water.

Peter got out of the boat and began walking out over the water towards Jesus. I imagine that the first steps Peter took were full of faith, with his eyes locked onto Jesus. Then, however, the Scripture says Peter saw the strong wind and waves and began to sink. Peter had taken his eyes off of Jesus and focused on his surroundings which caused him fear. Fear took the place of faith and he sank into the water.

Apply

When we take our eyes off of Jesus, we begin to sink into the water. We cannot walk out on water by ourselves. Jesus is calling us out of the boat, but we cannot do what He is calling us to do without keeping our eyes fixed on Him. When we lose our focus, our hearts and minds can become consumed with fear, anxiety, and doubt. Fight to keep your eyes fixed on Jesus. There are many distractions in this world; countless voices telling you what to do and who you are. Guard your heart and mind by choosing to listen to God's Word and trust His promises. Give Him your whole-hearted attention as you read His Word and learn about who He is and who He says you are. Your focused attention on God will actually rewire your brain so you can experience newness.

Pray

Lord, forgive me for getting caught up and spending my time focusing on things that lead me away from you. I pray that you would direct my thoughts and my heart back to you and your Word. Thank you that your Word is a light for my path that is always guiding me. I pray that you would help me to not get led astray from your will. Amen.

THE DEMON-POSSESSED MAN

Read

"Immediately there met Him out of the tombs, a man with an unclean spirit...no one could bind him, not even with chains...the chains had been pulled apart by him, and the shackles broken in pieces; neither could anyone tame him. And always, night and day, he was in the mountains and in the tombs, crying out and cutting himself with stones.

Then they came to Jesus, and saw the one who had been demon-possessed and had the legion, sitting and clothed and in his right mind."

-Mark 5:2-5, 15

Reflect

Can you imagine the misery that this man experienced for so long? Tormented by a legion of demons, struggling day and night, crying out, breaking out his bonds and cutting himself. The man endured this pain alone, cast out from his community to the tombs. No family, no medical attention, doomed to die in misery and isolation. But Jesus had other plans for him.

Mental illnesses like anxiety, depression, PTSD and others can cause similar symptoms, although maybe not to the same extreme. However, you may have experienced the torment mentally, physically, or spiritually when you battle mental illness, grief, trauma, and loss. Our minds can become a battlefield as we struggle in the fight to find peace or healing. Although there is purpose and fruit that can come during suffering, our merciful God offers healing to those who are experiencing an inconsolable mind.

Despite the extremity of the demon-possessed man's situation, one encounter with Jesus changed the course of his life forever. Jesus went out of his way, sought out the man, and commanded the demons out of him. This story demonstrates Jesus' heart for the one. The one who is outcast, forgotten, and overlooked. Jesus rescues those who are tormented, hopeless, and suffering. Jesus goes after God's children who have lost their way.

After word spread, people came to witness the man who was once tortured now sat fully clothed and with a sound mind. His encounter with Jesus changed him visibly, and the people were afraid because of the unbelievable miracle that had been done.

Apply

God's desire for you is the same. The Lord wants you to have a sound mind, free from torment and chaos. One encounter with Jesus can silence the panicked and anxious thoughts that may rule your life. One moment in God's presence can bring you stillness and wholeness that you will not find anywhere in this world. I searched for many years, high and low, for something that would relieve me of the perpetual darkness that took place in my mind. When your mind is in a hopeless place, that can dictate your actions and your life. But God, rich in mercy and grace, is willing and able to do abundantly more than we could ask or imagine. Seek Him wholeheartedly, and you will find that the more time you spend with Christ, the more whole your mind will become. The closer we draw near to God, the closer He draws near to us. Intimacy with God brings healing, redemption, and refreshment. Immerse your heart and mind in God's Word and worship Him. Seek, and you shall find. Knock, and the door will be answered. God does not abandon us in our time of need, and He does not overlook His children who are suffering.

Pray

God, I thank you for the wholeness that I can find in you. You see the pain and struggles I have endured. Thank you for not leaving me to suffer, and for bringing healing and redemption into my life. I pray for wholeness over my mind, body, and soul. Amen.

FEAR & FAITH

Read

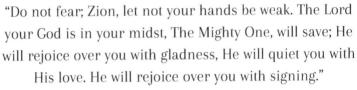

"Do not fear; Zion, let not your hands be weak. The Lord your God is in your midst, The Mighty One, will save; He will rejoice over you with gladness, He will quiet you with His love. He will rejoice over you with signing."
- Zephaniah 3:16-17

Reflect

When I think about calmness, I think about a quiet day at the ocean. There is nothing more than a gentle breeze and the water is still and glossy. The ocean is clear and peacefully rises and falls as the tide goes in and out. Calm.

When I think about fear, the picture is quite different. I see the ocean on a dark, stormy evening. The waves are powerful and destructive. There is much uncertainty and restlessness. The winds are whipping, creating more turmoil. Fear.

Fear is paralyzing. It causes weakness and doubt; our minds become like the waves on a stormy night, unstable and unclear. When fear consumes our hearts and our minds, it makes it almost impossible to make decisions or have any clarity of mind. You may feel as though you are drowning in the waves of pain and doubt as they beat relentlessly in your mind. How can we function when fear rules in our mind instead of faith? We can't. We will forever be tossed back and forth by the waves, never finding peace.

Apply

God does not desire us to live that way. With one word, He can quiet the storm in your mind. With His unconditional love, He can still the raging waves. But let us not make the same mistake the disciples made. While on the sea one night, a mighty storm came upon them and threatened to overtake the boat with the powerful waves. The disciples were overcome with fear and woke Jesus to tell Him they were at risk. Jesus simply arose and commanded the wind and waves to be still. But Jesus' concern was not about the storm, it was about the disciples' faith. He turned to them and said, "Why are you so fearful? How is it that you have no faith?" (Mark 4:35-41).

Fear is real. Sometimes, it can even be healthy, but God knows that fear can become crippling and destroy our faith. "Fear not" and "Do not be afraid" are said hundreds of times in the Bible. God understands our fear and has compassion for us. But Jesus is asking us the same question he asked the disciples that night they were overcome by fear, "Why are you so fearful? How is it that you have no faith?".

Do not feel condemned for not having faith. In Hebrews chapter 11, several people are named for being great examples of faith. When you take a closer look into their stories, they were imperfect people who made plenty of mistakes. But their faith is recognized because they lived their lives with the conviction that God fulfills His promises and they believed and obeyed His words. Scripture says that faith the size of a mustard seed (one of the smallest seeds ever) can move mountains. Take the smallest step of faith today. It could truly change everything for you. A step in faith is a step away from fear and towards Christ.

Pray

Jesus, forgive me for being overcome by fear. I pray that you would set me free from fear and help me to take steps of faith. I pray that you would be there for me when I am afraid and remind me that you are always with me. Amen.

TAKE THIS CUP

Read

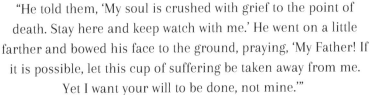

"He told them, 'My soul is crushed with grief to the point of death. Stay here and keep watch with me.' He went on a little farther and bowed his face to the ground, praying, 'My Father! If it is possible, let this cup of suffering be taken away from me. Yet I want your will to be done, not mine.'"

- Jesus, Matthew 26:38-39

Reflect

During times of pain and suffering, we often get on our knees and beg God to take our troubles away. Throughout the darkest times of my life, I begged God to give me relief, to rescue me out of the pit. When He didn't answer the way I wanted Him to, I became angry and resentful. God is all-powerful and all-knowing, yet there are times He seems so far away when I need Him.

A common misconception about God is that He doesn't understand suffering. Although it can be easy to believe this, Jesus' life proves otherwise. Jesus, the Son of God, came to earth fully human yet fully God to sacrifice Himself for mankind. The words of Jesus in the Garden of Gethsemane are heart wrenching. He knew the sacrifice He had to make, yet the weight of the burden overwhelmed Him. Jesus was crushed with grief. He begged God to take away the suffering He was enduring.

Jesus' plea to God is powerful. Despite the seemingly unbearable pain He was in and the incredible task that was before Him, Jesus wanted God's will to be done, not His own. Jesus, our Savior, laid Himself down for us, to fulfill the will of God. Jesus understood that God's will was to bring His children home to Him.

Apply

How often do we beg God for things to work out our way? How often do we come to God with our suffering and demand that He take it away? Many believe that once you become a Christian, everything should be perfect and free of trouble. When I gave my heart to Jesus at 17 years old, a great burden was lifted off of me. I felt as though I would never suffer again. A close look at God's Word illustrates the opposite. In fact, Jesus clearly stated that His disciples (including us today) would have troubles in this world. So why are we surprised when we suffer? We live in a dark, sinful world with confused and lost people. There is an enemy who is always trying to steal, kill, and destroy our lives.

While it feels like the odds are against us, the truth is that suffering brings us closer to the Lord. This is one of the hardest things to understand. Jesus suffered for us, so when we endure hardships, we become more like Him. During our struggles, we have a choice to either become bitter and resentful towards God for letting us suffer, or to draw near to God for shelter, strength, and comfort. We have a choice to calm our efforts to try to control our lives and instead let God hold us up. The fact that God Himself understands suffering on a personal level should bring us comfort. He actually suffers with us. If you struggle with the misconception that God is sitting on His throne watching you suffer alone, it is time to work through that. Learning about who God truly is as our Helper, Healer, and Comforter can change the way you suffer. No longer will you suffer alone or in vain. It's okay to feel that you cannot handle things on your own. It's okay to ask God to take the cup of suffering from you. Even Jesus did that. But in the end, are we obsessed with being free from temporary suffering, or do we want God's will to be done? When God doesn't answer the way you want Him to, what is your reaction? God's will may be that He rescues you immediately, or God's will may be that you have to endure for a little while. We have to strive to understand that God's will is greater and more perfect than anything we could come up with ourselves. Sometimes suffering is necessary to bring us closer to God, and there are amazing lessons and rewards at the end of it. God desires to love you and support you like a good father would.

Take steps of faith by asking God for His will to be done, not your own. The promise of the Bible is that when we lay ourselves down, we actually find life (Matthew 16:25). Even surrendering in the smallest way opens the door for God to work in amazing ways in your life.

Pray

Jesus, thank you for the sacrifice you made for me. I cannot begin to imagine the weight of the burden you carried to save God's children. I am set free because of what you did. Now, as I suffer, I know that I do not have to do it alone. Thank you for lifting me up and strengthening me through the trials of life. Help me to be patient to endure whatever it is that is before me, because I want your will to be done God, not my own. Forgive me for trying to control my circumstances. Guide me in your will God, because it is far better than what I can do in my own strength. I love you Lord. Amen.

TAMING THE TONGUE

Read

"The tongue has the power of life and death, and those who love it will eat its fruit."
- Proverbs 18:21

Reflect

This Scripture is one of many in the Bible that discusses the power of the tongue. The overall theme is that words have power, and the tongue can either set things on fire or bring life and encouragement. Consider the way that God created the world. He didn't do anything fancy, He simply spoke, and there was light. He spoke, and there was life. Reflect on Jesus' time on earth. During His ministry, He healed and set people free by declaring it in the name of the Father. When Jesus was tempted by the devil, He combated the deception with the Word of God.

Though this may seem dramatic, it is important to reflect on the influence of words in our lives. The phrase, "Sticks and stones may break my bones, but words will never hurt me" is common, yet inaccurate. Reflecting back on my own life, there have been instances where something was said over me that was devastating. On the other hand, I can look back and remember the encouragements and godly words that have been spoken over me that were powerful. I have experienced firsthand the life and death that words have brought into my life, and I'm sure you have as well. Words can create friendships, encourage others, and praise God. Words can also be used to harm others, destroy relationships, and deceive.

Apply

It is important to address the way we speak both to and about others. Do you encourage, build up, and give life to others with your tongue? Or do you gossip, deceive, or manipulate through your words? The reason it is so important to evaluate ourselves and the way we use our tongue is because it affects our entire lives. Negative talk comes from negative thoughts, which can lead to harmful behaviors and develop into a negative lens that you see everything through. Before you know it, you are stuck in a cynical cycle of negativity and death. Your life will be full of words that tear other people down to attempt to feel better about yourself. You may also struggle to see yourself in a positive way, and even talk negatively to yourself. "I am such an idiot", "I hate the way I look", "I can never do anything right" or "Nobody loves me because I always screw up" are statements that we say to ourselves when we are stuck in a negative pattern of thinking and speaking. We can get lost in a perpetual cycle of speaking death over others and ourselves.

To break out of this, it is crucial that you begin to acknowledge the tendencies you may have. Do you have a habit of speaking negatively about others? Do you tend to speak sarcastically, taking jabs meant to harm, but you cover it up as a joke? Or do you struggle with negative thoughts about yourself? Do you look in the mirror and think positively, or do you speak harmful things over who you are or your appearance? Once you begin to notice these negative patterns of thinking or speaking, you can start catching the words before they leave your mouth. Then, practice surrendering those things to God. God does not expect you to be able to do this on your own. We can spend years in a cycle of negativity which can be difficult to break out of. That's why God offers the Spirit to help convict you when you need it and enable you to exercise self-control.

Finally, practice speaking Scripture over yourself and others. Ask God to provide you with encouraging words for other people. Pray that God would help you to see yourself and others as His children, made in His image.

The Word of God holds power, and when you use it as a weapon against the enemy who brings death and negativity, he stands no chance. As you make these changes to your words and thoughts, watch the kingdom of God enter your life, bringing healing and light instead of death.

Pray

God, help make me aware of the words that I speak to myself and others. Point out the negative thought patterns that I have that lead to destructive words. Holy Spirit, give me conviction and give me self-control so that I can tame my tongue. Give me encouraging words for others and for myself. Help me to keep Scripture in my heart so that I can speak the power of God's Word over my circumstances and my life. Amen.

THE WAR WITHIN OUR MINDS

Read

"I have discovered this principle of life- that when I want to do what is right, I inevitably do what is wrong. I love God's law with all my heart. But there is another power within me that is at war with my mind. This power makes me a slave to the sin that is still within me. Oh, what a miserable person I am! Who will free me from this life that is dominated by sin and death? Thank God! The answer is in Jesus Christ our Lord."
- The Apostle Paul, Romans 7:21-25

Reflect

The Apostle Paul, one of the most influential figures in the Bible, radically transformed by God Himself, wrote about the war he experienced in his mind. The war was the battle between his flesh and God's Word. Paul loved God's word and wanted nothing more than to serve Him with everything he had. Paul knew what was right, what was wrong, and what God wanted from him. Yet, the mighty man of God struggled. He wrestled with light and darkness. He stated that he knew what was right and he wanted to do it, yet he fell short. Earlier in Romans (Chapter 3:23), Paul wrote that all have sinned and fall short of the glory of God. Why? Because humans have a sinful nature that battles to take control and lead them into darkness.

This struggle is very real for us as Christians. The problem is, when we fall short of what we know we should do, we hide from God like Adam and Eve did in the garden. We become ashamed, guilty, and condemned. We become angry and look for someone or something to blame instead of ourselves. Sometimes, we even give up trying because we are tired of feeling so shameful about the way we live. So, instead of working towards the way we know we should, we decide to give in to our flesh and live according to our sinful desires. After failing time and time again, it often feels easier to embrace sinful living rather than dealing with the guilt of coming up short. We justify this by believing it is easier to give up than to fight for living right by God. This is the road to a hard heart.

Apply

Despite our shortcomings, we do not have to be a slave to sin. Paul cried out, "Who will save me from this life that is dominated by sin and death?" How does he reply to himself? "Thank God! The answer is Jesus Christ our Lord." Jesus is the answer to his cry for freedom. Jesus is the answer to our desperate need to be saved from our flesh that leads us into darkness.

How is Jesus the answer? He died on a cross, bearing the weight of sin, and rose again defeating it. That means that when we surrender to Him, Christ can deliver us from the sin that brings death.

However, we are still humans, and we still live in a sinful world. This means that the enemy will try his best to tempt us to fall into sin again. That is why it is a constant battle. Once you know Jesus, you know you can be free, but you are engaged in a continuous fight against your flesh that wants to act a different way.

The implications of this revelation that Paul had is this: we are human. We are not perfect. Every single one of us will fall short. We will make mistakes and we will have to deal with the consequences of our choices. The question is this: what will we do when we fall? Do we become ashamed, angry, or condemned? Do we run from God in fear that He is disappointed or angry with us? Or do we turn to our loving Father, asking for forgiveness and help to change our ways? The church doesn't always do a good job addressing this. Many people feel that God's expectations are too high, and that it's impossible to meet them. The truth is, it is impossible on our own.

In our own strength, we will battle and lose. But if we are willing to humble ourselves before God and ask for His strength, we can walk in the victory that Jesus won when He rose from the grave.

It is inevitable that you will make mistakes as you walk through life. That is part of being human.

You may make wrong decisions, give in to your flesh, and experience the battle in your mind between light and darkness. But God sees your heart. If you truly love Him and you constantly come back to Him with repentance and humbleness, God can work in amazing ways in your life. You can experience freedom from the snares of sin that can so easily trip you up. You can walk in the life that Jesus died for you to have. Do not let fear, shame, or guilt hold you back from going to the Father for forgiveness and guidance. God does not demand perfection; He only wants your whole heart.

Pray

Jesus, I constantly battle between light and darkness. I am sorry for the times I have given in to my flesh and turned away from you. I pray that you would soften my heart and give me the strength to choose you instead of sin. I rebuke the enemy in Jesus name from making me feel shameful and condemned about my mistakes. I thank you Jesus for the price you paid so that I can be free from condemnation. I give you my whole heart God, and I ask that you would help me to repent and turn away from my sins so that I can live in your freedom. Amen.

SEEKING FELLOWSHIP

Read

"Every day they continued to meet together in the temple courts. They broke bread in their homes and ate together with glad and sincere hearts, praising God and enjoying the favor of all the people. And the Lord added to their number daily those who were being saved."

- Acts 2:46-47

"Not giving up meeting together, as some are in the habit of doing, but encouraging one another- and all the more as you see the Day approaching."

- Hebrews 10:25

Reflect

Isolation is a dangerous place to be. Depression, anxiety, grief, and other struggles can make you feel completely drained all the time, with no capacity to engage in anything social. Although there have been several times in my life I did not have the physical or emotional energy to be around anyone, the more I gave in to isolation, the harder it was to get out of it. The enemy uses isolation as a way to separate you from other believers so it is easier to trap you and deceive you. How do predators like wolves and lions succeed in hunting their prey? They separate their prey from the pack so they can take them down easier. Unfortunately, the same is true for us. We are vulnerable when we are alone. There is a battle raging in our minds- it can be hard to know what is from God and what is not, or what is truth and what is a lie. When I am alone and my thoughts are out of control, I am very susceptible to the enemy's attacks on my faith. The longer I am in isolation, the easier it is for me to believe lies about myself and about God. I become fearful, overwhelmed, guilty, and trapped by my feelings that lead me astray.

Apply

After Jesus ascended into heaven, the disciples were sent on their mission to proclaim the Gospel. During this time, Scripture illustrates the importance they placed on continually meeting with one another, sharing meals, and lifting one another up. Their ministry prospered because of their devotion to one another and the Lord.

We often overlook the importance of fellowship. I am guilty of this, as I have always wanted to keep my feelings and struggles to myself and do things on my own. It took several times of me hitting rock bottom and being lifted up by others for me to realize I am not meant to do life alone, and neither are you. In your most vulnerable moments, it is scary to reach out to others for support and encouragement. It takes huge steps of humility to lay down your pride and bear your soul to someone. But the support you will receive from the family of God is crucial to your walk with Christ. One point I want to make is this: be careful who you surround yourself with. Fellowship is the gathering with fellow believers. While you should not exclude those who do not know Christ from the family of God, these are not the people you should surround yourself with when you are in need of godly support and guidance. Sometimes you need to hear the truth in love, and sometimes your thoughts or feelings need to be challenged if they do not line up with God's Word.

Therefore, seek fellowship, whether you feel like it or not. Even if it is in small doses, like gathering with one or two believers who care for you and want to lift you up. Do not hide your suffering from others. Ask God to give you the strength to ask for support and love when you need it the most. Do not believe the lies of the enemy who will try to keep you isolated. People are not perfect, and they may not always say the right things. But being surrounded by love and acceptance regardless of your circumstances is empowering and will enable you to find strength in the Lord.

Pray

Lord, thank you that I am not alone in my battles. Even though there are times I feel isolated, I pray you would send people to lift me up. I pray you would help me to be vulnerable with the people in my life you have provided me with. Help me to lay down my pride and ask for help when I need it. I rebuke the enemy in Jesus name from trying to keep me isolated to speak lies to me. God, I pray that you would send people who do not tell me what I want to hear, but speak the truth in love. Amen.

DAY TWENTY-ONE

HEART, MIND AND SOUL

Read

" 'Teacher, which is the greatest commandment in the Law?' Jesus replied: 'Love the Lord your God with all your heart and with all your soul and with all your mind.' This is the first and greatest commandment.' "

- Matthew 22:36-37

Reflect

In these verses, Jesus was being questioned by the Pharisees. Speaking with authority and being straightforward, Jesus proclaimed the greatest commandment: to love God with all our hearts, souls, and minds. In other words, love God with *everything* you have.

In Christianity, we often lose sight of this. It is easy to get caught up in the way we should look, talk, and act as Christians. Those things can be important, but they should not take precedence over the first and greatest commandment. Instead of trying to fix our behavior or our appearance (as the Pharisees were mainly concerned with), we need to whole-heartedly surrender to God. This begins with learning who Christ is and how to love Him with everything we have.

The heart, soul, and mind work together harmoniously to love God. They should not be separate, although we sometimes treat them like they are. To truly love God, all three of these components need to be taught to understand God's heart and how to completely surrender to Him.

Apply

To teach our hearts, souls, and minds to love Christ as a whole, we need to address each component. The *heart*, representing emotions, can easily lead us astray. Learning self-control, arguably one of the most difficult areas for humans, will enable us to love God *despite* our emotions. This means that although our hearts may take us on a rollercoaster ride of emotions, we can always come back to the steadfast love of God. Feelings are temporary, but many times we act on them as if they are truth. It is crucial that we write Scripture on our hearts as the only truth, and teach our feelings and emotions to be regulated by it.

The *soul* is our innermost being that can only find freedom and rest in Christ. Jesus warns in Matthew 16:26 that we risk losing our souls when we seek to gain the whole world. To take care of our souls, we must know and accept Christ as Savior and reject our old ways of living so we can live eternally with Him. All throughout the book of Psalms, the psalmists cry out with all their souls their love for God. A soul that is alive is one that knows God intimately.

Finally, the *mind*. This is the component that is so easily overlooked. Our restless minds are filled with constant thoughts that can either suck us into a deep pit or lead us to a deeper relationship with God. As part of the theme of this devotional, we need to emphasize the importance of promoting mental health in our lives because we cannot truly love God without it. We must fill our minds with God's truth and an awareness of who we are in Christ so we can love God fully.

It is amazing what happens when we focus on submitting our hearts, minds and souls to God instead of trying to fix our behavior to be a good Christian. When your heart, soul, and mind are fixed on the Lord, it causes your behavior to change. A deep, intimate knowledge and relationship with the Lord changes your thoughts, attitudes, and behaviors because you love Him and He loves you. Let us return to the greatest commandment to lead us in our Christian walk instead of attempting to bandage our lives up in an attempt to fix ourselves to be a follower.

Pray

God, I am eternally thankful for who you are and what you have done for me. I pray that you would help me to continually submit my heart, soul, and mind to you so I can love you with everything I have. You are a perfect, holy, loving God that deserves everything I have and more. Teach me to regulate my emotions and write your Scripture on my heart so that I am not led astray by my feelings. Help me to refrain from giving my soul away for the things of this world but to instead submit it to you so I can live eternally because of your sacrifice. Jesus, I pray for healing, newness, and peace in my mind. Help me to care for myself mentally so I can love you completely. Amen.

Notes

1. Kwon, H., & Kim, Y. (2019). Perceived emotion suppression and culture: Effects on psychological well-being. *International Journal of Psychology*, 54(4), 448-453.

2. Wong, D. W., Hall, K. R., Justice, C. A., & Hernandez, L. W. (2015). *Counseling individuals through the lifespan.* SAGE Publications, Inc.

3. Simmons, R. T., Lilley, S. C., & Kuhnley, A. K. (2020). *Introduction to counseling: Integration of faith, professional identity, and clinical practice.* Kendall Hunt Publishing Company.

4. Miyoshi, T., Tanioka, K., Yamamoto, S., Yadohisa, H., Hiroyasu, T., & Hiwa, S. (2019). Revealing changes in brain functional networks caused by focused-attention meditation using Tucker3 clustering. *Frontiers in Human Neuroscience, 13*, 473-473.

TO CONTINUE THE CONVERSATION

about mental & spiritual health

Connect with me at:

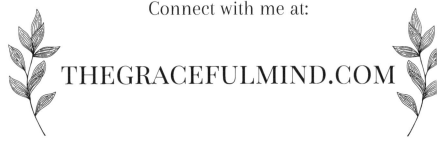

THEGRACEFULMIND.COM

ACKNOWLEDGEMENTS

My journey towards mental wellness is full of ups and downs. Thankfully, I have never been alone during any of it.

Thank you to my sweet husband Brian, for being a steadfast encourager throughout our entire relationship. You fill my life with laughter and love.

To all my amazing friends- you have seen me at my worst and at my best, and you have never left my side. Thank you for loving me and cultivating a bravery in me to follow Christ with all my heart. To Megan- you have been crucial to the development of this book. Thank you for being my cheerleader, editor, and advocate.

To my family- thank you for cheering me on during every season of life. I pray you are encouraged by reading this book.

To my Liberty church family- thank you for accepting me as I am and helping me form such a strong foundation in the Lord. You gave me room to grow in Christ and discover my calling.

To Pastor Jamie and family- thank you for giving me such a love for God's Word and showing me how to walk it out.

To my Rise family- You are overcomers in Christ, and you are going to change the world one day. I am thankful to be a part of the family.

To Karla- thank you teaching me how to work on my mental health and for inspiring me to share what I've learned.

Made in the USA
Monee, IL
24 September 2021

78733890R00037